WILD ABOUT
Twickenham

FROM RUGBY TO THE RIVER

By Andrew Wilson

Sponsored by

Milestone &
Collis
Chartered Surveyors
Est.1890

For Pam and Gerry, my in-laws, who sadly both died this summer.
Great supporters of my books, whilst still well enough Gerry proofed my first couple of books.

Clockwise from top left: The river front, Twickenham Stadium, St. Mary's Church and Church Street

Opposite: Eel Pie Island Bridge across the Thames

Contents

NEW FEATURE

Local walks

New to the Wild About Series are the local walks allowing you to really get to know the area as depicted in each book. *(See page 202)*

Welcome to Wild About Twickenham

Welcome to my latest collection of photographs. I have been coming to this area for some years, especially since we got our dog. There are so many wonderful places to walk and I shall miss the regular trips across Richmond Park to the Ham Lands, where I would pick up Hammerton's Ferry and start my exploration of your wonderful town. With the World Cup coming in 2015, it was suggested to me by Bruce Lyons of Crusader Travel that his town would be a great place to capture with my camera and he wasn't wrong. For the benefit of my Springer, I always plot my routes via places I can let her off the lead, but there is so much more to the area than just the open spaces: you have the stunning architecture of places like Strawberry Hill House and Marble Hill

and then a feast of events throughout the year, particularly in the summer, including a packed two week festival. Knowing some of the larger open spaces it is still a delight when you discover new ones, from tiny places like Oak Lane Cemetery to the splendour of the St Margarets Pleasure Gardens, where I was kindly given special access. I have loved working on this latest collection and I hope you enjoy it.

As with all my books, they take time and effort to produce and would never happen without the help and assistance of others. Firstly, I would like to thank Antony Robson and all the staff of local estate agents Milestone & Collis and Colin Squire of Squire's Garden Centres for kindly agreeing to sponsor my book. Antony's main office is in Church Street and I was always greeted with friendly smiles from his staff, especially Jacqui, whenever I

dropped by. I am very much at ease with my camera but writing is not so much my thing, so I am grateful to local historian Ed Harris for providing my introduction and further help on some of the background to some of the places of note. In this I was helped immeasurably towards the end by a graduate intern from Roehampton University, Jessica Dean, who helped pull all this text together. Thank you also to local artist Stephen King for providing such a splendid and colourful watercolour map of the area. Then there is my designer, Tim Ball and colour expert, Paul Sherfield, who help ensure that all this work is not in vain and looks fabulous on the page.

My books take well over a year to produce and I meet many people along the way who have helped or contributed and unfortunately space does not allow me to mention you all. As much as possible I try and make reference to people in relevant editorial within the book but please forgive me if I have inadvertently missed you out, it's nothing personal. With such a rich canvass to work from but only so much time, there are also places to which I would have liked to have visited, the local allotments for instance, and also one or two places that I did but have no room to feature, The Rifleman pub for instance, which looked great.

The last 18 months has been a delight being a visitor to your town and I hope you like my travelogue.

Andrew Wilson, October 2014

Left: Josie, my Springer Spaniel and constant companion, outside Twickenham Museum on the Embankment. The museum is open on Tuesday, Saturday and Sunday and is a wonderful treasure trove of information on the local area. Entry is free but they very much welcome donations. Another good source of local information is the Borough of Twickenham Local History Society – *www.botlhs.co.uk*

Opposite: Swans swim past the White Swan pub on the river, past the Ham Lands on the other bank, and onwards to Eel Pie Island.

Twickenham

A SHORT HISTORY OF THE AREA
by Ed Harris

Be it boating at Henley, tennis at Wimbledon or football at Wembley, Twickenham looms large as part of the quintessentially British calendar of sporting and social events. Boasting the largest stadium in the world devoted to the game of rugby, its 82,000 spectator capacity has also continued Twickenham's long association with popular music giants the likes of Rod Stewart and The Rolling Stones who once played on the legendary Eel Pie Island together with some of Britain's greatest jazz, rock and R&B musicians including Kenny Ball, David Bowie and Pink Floyd. Sadly, the hotel where they played has gone, burned down in a mysterious fire in 1971.

Twickenham is home to one of the oldest surviving film studios in the country. Situated towards the east of the town, at St Margarets, the first film produced here was a silent called The House of Temperley shot in 1913. Of the many movie milestones thereafter, the films that attract the most attention are The Beatles' trilogy *A Hard Day's Night*, *Help!* and *Let It Be*.

Masses of artefacts belonging to the oldest known local residents dating back to 3,000 BC were uncovered in 1966 from underneath the car park between Church Street and The Embankment. Thousands of bison, wild ox, woolly rhinoceros and mammoth bones dating back much further, to 41,000 BC, were unearthed along the riverside in the late 19th century during the laying of drains. But it's not until the 8th century AD that we find the hand of man writ large in a charter describing 'Twicanhom' as a tract of land bounded by what are now the Rivers Thames to the south and the Crane to the north.

The Crane valley continues its open course through Twickenham offering a selection pleasant green places, and in particular a nature reserve set among the romantic ruins of the old gunpowder mills that once rocked the landscape for miles around with its thunderous explosions.

There were at least two Roman settlements in Twickenham. After the Saxons came the Normans. Although not recorded individually in the Domesday survey of 1086, Twickenham was included with Whitton, Isleworth and Hounslow. St Mary's Church rests on its natural promontory by the riverside, as did its Saxon forebear to represents the start of the medieval built landscape. Richard, Earl of Cornwall, enclosed a large tract of natural heathland in 1277 to create Twickenham

Left: Twickenham has changed a lot over the centuries, but as you can see from the pictures on this and the following pages, many of the buildings have remained the same. Taken looking west along Church Street, just outside the Twickenham Town Club, many of the same structures can be seen. The 20th and early 21st century cards used have been kindly supplied by a local historian and resident. If you wish to know more about his collection of historic cards, please contact the publisher.

Below: Twickenham Town Club on Church Street celebrates its 150th anniversary in 2015, and will be organising plenty of events, including a very visual presence at the Twickenham Festival. Previously a Gentlemen's Club, it now opens its doors to all genders.

Park where Francis Bacon came to live. By the time Moses Glover produced his famous map of 1635, Twickenham had become a thriving riverside town complete with its own brewery, brick fields and with picturesque Church Street its main highway.

By the 18th century Twickenham had grown to become a favoured haunt for the houses of the nobility, poets, writers and artists as well as merchants and other wealthy residents. Free from the stifling pollution of London, Twickenham was ideally situated along what was then London's superhighway, The Thames. The satirist and poet, Alexander Pope, came to Twickenham in 1719 and lived in his riverside villa in Cross Deep until his death in 1744. An influential figure in the development of landscape gardening only his famed grotto survives.

Collector and antiquary, essayist and novelist, Horace Walpole, bought a small house nearby in Strawberry Hill in 1747 which he enlarged, embellished and decorated in a style that became known as Strawberry Hill gothic. It survives as the most stunning example of Twickenham's golden age and is now a world heritage site. Other notable figures of the period include Henry Fielding, briefly resident in Twickenham at the time he was writing

Below: Cross Deep, Pope's Villa and Radnor House School

'Tom Jones', the artists Samuel Scott and Thomas Hudson, with Sir Godfrey Kneller a near neighbour in Whitton, and poets Paul Whitehead and Richard Owen Cambridge.

The literary and artistic connections continued into the 19th century with arguably Britain's greatest landscape painter, J.M.W. Turner, who designed his own house in Sandycombe Road as a country retreat for himself and his father and where a Trust is now established to restore the house to its original appearance. Charles Dickens spent the summer of 1838 in St Margarets and features Twickenham in several novels. In the 1850s R D Blackmore, author of 'Lorna Doone', was a master at the Wellesley House School on the Hampton Road and Alfred Lord Tennyson lived on Montpelier Row, a stunning terrace of fine Georgian townhouses enjoying beautiful views of historic Marble Hill Park with its bone-white Palladian villa originally built for Henriette Howard, the mistress of King George II in 1729.

West along the riverside from Marble Hill Park towards Twickenham town centre are two stunning buildings both with royal associations. The baroque Octagon Room set into a secluded woodland setting was designed by the renowned 18th century architect James Gibbs as a garden pavilion for the substantial mansion commissioned by James Johnson, Secretary for Scotland, which was demolished by a firm of ballast and gravel merchants in 1926.

York House dates back to the 17th century but has been added to in subsequent centuries. It was acquired by Twickenham Borough Council in 1924 and since 1965 it has been the municipal offices of the London Borough of Richmond upon Thames, housing the Mayor's parlour and committee rooms. Major restoration and renovation was undertaken by its last private occupier, Sir Ratan J. Tata, a wealthy industrialist. He's chiefly remembered for

King Street   Twickenham

the risqué Naked Ladies Italianate fountain he had installed in the fine riverside gardens.

From 1800 to 1807 the Duc d'Orleans and his two brothers decided upon Twickenham to live out their exile. The Duc returned in 1815, this time living in Orleans house. During the 1860s three of the late Duc's sons were living in the area, one of them at Orleans House and one grandson at York House where fleur de lys detail marks an extension made by the Orleanist pretender while living there from 1896 to 1900.

The coming of the railway to Twickenham in 1848 was a significant factor in the rapid growth of the town. As grander developments such as Trafalgar Square (now Road) began to cover the fields and open countryside west of the working class clusters, so former great estates were sold off for mass housing that led to a seven-fold increase in the population of Twickenham from 3,000 in 1800 to 21,000 in 1901. Trams were introduced in Twickenham in 1903 and buses in 1910. The increase in road traffic throughout the 1920s and 30s was such that it led to the construction of the first bridge across The Thames at Twickenham in 1932, which, in turn, offered developers direct access from the capital to the area's extensive market garden, orchard and nurserylands.

Ed Harris *e.harris510@btinternet.com*

Below: Looking east down York Street
Bottom left: The Rugby Store, York Street

THE KINGSWAY, TWICKENHAM

S 5893

Twickenham

Twickenham Stadium

Kneller Hall A316

St Margarets

Cole Park

Pleasure Gdns

The Avenue East Twickenham

St Margarets Road

Cambridge Gardens

Whitton

Harlequins The Stoop

Richmond Road

Chertsey Road

River Crane

Twickenham

York House Gdns

Marble Hill House

Orleans House

River Thames

Crane Valley

Nature reserve

Twickenham Green

Heath Road Station

Cross Deep

King St

Ham House

Ham Riverside Lands

Strawberry Hill Golf Course

Strawberry Hill House

Strawberry Hill

This map was kindly supplied to us by local artist, Stephen King, who lives just off Twickenham Green. It is not meant to be absolutely to scale but to give the reader a fun introduction to the area and some of the places covered in this book. He can be contacted via his website: www.stephenkinggallery.com

11

Riverside

Twickenham is one of luckiest areas in South West London, as in addition to its picturesque and newly restored riverfront it also has its very own island. This beautiful area of Greater London, as the river makes its route from the centre of town and travels towards the countryside, has been very desirable land for centuries; in the 1700s many grand houses were built here because of the close proximity to the city whilst still being upstream from the pollution.

A lot of money has been recently spent to upgrade the front, with the inclusion of the new Jubilee Gardens, built on the former open air swimming pool in 2012. This together with the other works that have going on across the town centre will help to make this a magnet for all those visitors expected to flock here for the Rugby World Cup in September 2015.

Previous page: The seagulls next to Eel Pie Island are busy looking for lunch from the people who regularly feed the birds.

This spread: Residents and visitors need to keep an eye on the tide, because at particularly high tides the Embankment and the Boardwalk flood. Slightly impractical, but when it creates beautiful scenes like this, it's hard to mind.

Overleaf: Watching the sunrise from Eel Pie Island bridge is a beautiful sight.

This page: Commuters from Eel Pie Island cross the river in the fog, silhouetted on the bridge. Before the bridge was built, travellers had to ferry themselves across in boats, probably not always a pleasant job on a foggy and cold day like this.

This spread: The sun sets west along the river. The birds, unmoved by the beautiful sight, continue to hunt for their dinner.

This pair of swans were very protective of their territory.

Opposite top and bottom right: Previously known as the Queens Head Hotel, due to the owners weird, or you could say barmy, tradition of assembling their Christmas Tree upside down it was renamed the Barmy Arms in the 1970s. It has played host to many iconic performers over the years, from such bands as Genesis, Rod Stewart and The Rolling Stones.

Opposite bottom left: The Mary Wallace Theatre, just back from the riverfront, is the home of the Richmond Shakespeare Society, a highly-respected amateur dramatic society.

This page top and bottom left: Strand House on the alleyway just back from the Embankment is a Grade II listed property, and was built in 1705. The beautiful wisteria growing up the face of the property add a touch of colour to the Queen Anne style house.

In November, this stretch of the Thames has an extremely low tide, but this isn't natural, it's man made! Named the annual Draw Off, the locks are manipulated to make the water levels go as low as possible so that the river bed can be excavated and examined, with many joining in the fun to see what they can find. At this point, you can walk across to Eel Pie Island, if you wear some waterproof trousers.

In the last few years, the face of the riverfront has changed significantly, as they've refurbished the whole area. After removing the old Horse Chestnuts, they created whole new gardens for the public to enjoy.

Bottom left: The old riverfront before the redevelopments

Sailing

Using the Thames for leisure sailing around Twickenham is a fairly recent practise; only since the construction of Richmond's Half Tide Lock in 1894 were the water levels reliable enough to sail year round on, especially in the summer months. In 1894 the Swan Sailing club was founded, named after their meeting place in the Swan Inn, though when Twickenham Council purchased York House, they moved into the boathouse on the grounds and changed their name to the current Twickenham Yacht club.

During WWII, many members joined the forces or, in the case of older members or those on essential war work, joined the Emergency River Service. Some boats were also sent to help in evacuation efforts, and like some of the men, were never to return.

Expansions and improvements have been made on the boathouse since the move to accommodate for the growing popularity of the club and of the sport in general. Regular open days are held to encourage new members to join, and during the summer they race every Sunday and Wednesday between Eel Pie Island and Marble Hill Park.

Left: Thanks to club members Bob, for organising my visit one beautiful summer's morning and for Olwen who kindly took me out in their support boat.

Top right: The club

This spread: On beautiful days like this, its easy to see why sailing is such a popular hobby for Twickenham residents.

Next page and overleaf: Cruise ships go on the south (left) side of Eel Pie Island, and Twickenham lies on the north, with Twickenham Yacht Club, York House Gardens and St Mary's Church all visible from the water.

St Mary's Church

The grounds of St Mary's Church have been used as a church for centuries. The grey tower on the church is made from Medieval Kentish Rag Stone, which dates back to the 15thC, though evidence points towards a church being here since the early 13thC. In 1713, the vicar of the time expressed concern that the church was structurally unsound and would collapse, moving services out and beginning to plan emergency reconstruction, but three days later on the 9th April during the night, the building collapsed.

James John, architect of Orleans House, worked with painter Sir Godfrey Kneller, church warden of the church at the time, to design and build the new Neoclassical redbrick building that survives today, incorporating the Rag Stone tower with the Tuscan pilasters and pediments. There are eight bells in the tower, one from the 16thC, three from the 17thC and four from the 18thC, while unfortunately the Victorian stained glass windows were destroyed by a nearby bomb during the blitz. Walking through the church, you can truly see history progress here, with a brass plaque from 1443, and a stone slab marking the grave of Alexander Pope.

Today, the church meets several times a week, and maintains a very busy calendar, always welcoming old and new visitors alike on this ancient site.

Twickenham has a close relationship with the river, especially at high tide. Every day, the water levels rise over Church Street and Flood Lane, meaning the same view at different times can look completely different.

On the wall in front of the church is a small plaque (inset) marking the high tide level of the flood in 1774, eight foot above the road level.

The beautiful cherry trees outside the church light up the grounds. The doorway from the rag stone medieval tower gets coated in blossom in the spring, and brilliant orange and red leaves in the autumn.

Right: From the top of the bell tower there's a wonderful view of Eel Pie Island, with the rowing club and boat yard, and the Ham Lands on the other side of the Thames, stretching into the distance.

Thanks to Charlotte West, church warden of St Mary's, and Norman Edwards, chief bell ringer, for kindly letting me up the tower to take this picture and one or two others in the book.

Eel Pie Island

Eel Pie Island is only accessible by boat, or, as of 1957, by foot via the footbridge across the Thames. This tiny island has been home to many notable people, such as the original Doctor, William Hartnell, in the BBC's Doctor Who. The Eel Pie Island Hotel played host to a whole generation of iconic musicians, with The Who, Yardbirds, Mick Jagger and Rod Stewart playing in the jazz club. Arthur Chisnall, founder of the club, set up the venue as a personal social experiment for himself; interested in how those born at the end of WWII would develop, he created a little world for them with the freedom to grow, inadvertently creating one of the most iconic venues of the era. The hotel burned down in 1971, and the island has since become privately owned, including many artists who open the island twice a year for gallery viewings.

Walking around the island, it's hard to miss the fact that this is an artists community. Brightly painted houses and sheds appear around every corner, with fun signs and artwork decorating the gardens.

Left: Eel Pie Boatyard is a small, family run business based on the North bank. It offers moorings, and repairs many types of boats, though encourages people to try DIY work. They rent out workshops to small businesses, artists and craftspeople on the island.

Opposite top right: Amongst the organisations found in the office complex on the island is The South West London Environment Network, one of many charities housed here. SWLEN works hard to encourage local people and organisations to work together to protect and improve the environment.

Opposite top left: Trevor Baylis OBE (left) is possibly the island's most famous current occupant and amongst its many accomplishments its possibly the invention of his wind-up radio that he will be best remembered. He is sitting here with Con O'Brien (right), town centre manager for Richmond.

Twickenham Rowing Club

The first boathouse for the Twickenham Rowing Club was a floating structure and was moored off of Eel Pie Island in the 1860s, and after sinking a few times a fixed Boathouse was built on the island in the 1870s. The first president of the club was Henri, Duc D'Aumale, fifth son of Louis Phillipe I, King of France, who lived in Twickenham's York House in the mid 1800s.

Many thanks to the club for allowing me to take some of these pictures, especially the ones from the island.

Twickenham Rowing Club, the slowest ever winning crew of the Thames Cup at Henley Royal Regatta, practices along this stretch of the river, sporting their bright team colours of navy and magenta.

Sunday mornings at
Twickenham Rowing Club,
are always very popular.

Twickenham Festival

For two weeks every June, the annual Twickenham Festival celebrate the town, welcoming visitors, supporting the local businesses and encouraging a community atmosphere. The events incorporate many different parts of the Village, The River Thames Eel Pie Island, Twickenham Green and reminding the public of its musical connection and rich heritage. A tug of war opens the festival on a Friday, and events like the Orleans Gallery Carnival & pageant, Church Street 'Goes Green', river cruises, St Mary's Church fair, the Best Banger in the Borough competition and Twickenham's now famous Al Fresco Dining enticing everyone out onto the streets.

It not only supports local businesses, but is also supported by a number of them. Twickenham Town Business Association is especially involved with the green Church Street, The Eel Pie opens the Tug of War, and Crusader Travel offers pre-paid holidays as part of the raffle. Other supporters include The Cabbage Patch, the RFU, Stone Rowe Brewer Solicitors, Green 4 Ever, Try Twickenham and London Farmers' Market.

Tug of War

The festival is opened with a tug of war outside the Eel Pie Pub, and in 2014 eight teams representing different local businesses competed, including the staff of the pub as one of the first competitors.

Opposite top left: Second in line is Penny, manageress of the Eel Pie Pub.

Opposite bottom: Thanks to the staff of the Eel Pie Pub for allowing me into the flat above to take this photo.

Opposite: Twickenham Yacht club hold an open day to let people test the waters and see if they might have an undiscovered passion or talent for the sport.

This page: Twickenham Festival centres around Church Street, closing the street for several events such as the Tug of War, 'Goes Green', French Market, and a Lunchtime concert, as well as the regular summer feature of the Al Fresco dining.

St Mary's Church Fair

On the first Saturday of the Festival, St Mary's church opens its doors to the public for a classic church fair, with games to play and prizes to win. Proceeds from the day go to Mercy Ships, providing medical care to third world countries, and Mission to Seafarers, keeping the world's sailors and fishermen afloat.

Children slung off their jackets and hooked ducks for prizes throughout the day, and stayed well fed by Dave and Dave whilst Mary and Cath sold their wares.

Church Street 'Goes Green' and the Carnival

Opposite: Until the end of the 19thC, the Twickenham area was 40 per cent market gardens, supplying London with fruit, vegetables and flowers. Twickenham Town Business Association celebrated this for the second year in a row, carpeting Church Street with fake grass to recapture the countryside atmosphere feel of the town.

This page: On the second weekend of the Festival, Orleans House Gardens entertained the Twickenham Carnival, which included a procession through the town headed by our mayor Cllr. Jane Boulton with floats, music and dancing. This year's theme was the tercentenary of the Hanoverian succession hence the lively costumes.

Jubilee Gardens

Jubilee Gardens on the riverfront are one of Twickenham's newest enhancements, opened in 2012 for the Diamond Jubilee. This site used to be a outdoor swimming pool, still marked by the old diving board (bottom right).

Top: The Best Banger competition was held in Jubilee Gardens during the festival, and was won by Armstrong's in St Margarets (page 155).

Bottom Left: This wonderful floral map, put up in 2013, was created by Emily Allchurch and pupils from Orleans Park School.

Dragonboat Racing

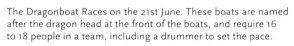

The Dragonboat Races on the 21st June. These boats are named after the dragon head at the front of the boats, and require 16 to 18 people in a team, including a drummer to set the pace.

It is one of many events put on throughout the year by Twickenham Alive, a local social enterprise – *www.twickenhamalive.com*

Rugby

Twickenham Stadium is the largest rugby stadium in the world, the second largest stadium in England, and the fifth largest in Europe, making Twickers the central hub for the sport, with almost all home games played here.

After the successes of the sold out games at Crystal Palace, the RFU decided to build a stadium solely for Rugby, and started building in 1907. The ten acre area of land was previously used to grow cabbages, leading to the ground being affectionately nicknamed 'The Cabbage Patch', and a pub of the same name. The first game played was between Harlequin and Richmond on the 2nd October 1909.

The anthem for the stadium is *Swing Low, Sweet Chariot*, first sung in the last match of the 1988 season, when England won spectacularly, for the performance of the first black player in 80 years, Chris Oti. On Oti's second try, a group of students from a nearby school sung the song associated with the Underground Railroad freedom movement for American slaves, and the crowd soon joined in, leading to the tradition today.

Opposite page: This wonderful bronze sculpture was unveiled outside the stadium in 2010 and was created by Gerald Laing. With The World Cup I dare say this fantastic piece of art will feature in many visitors photographic memories.

Twickenham Stadium

Opposite: No day at the rugby is complete without a good drink, and Twickenham stadium makes sure to provide. The massive white tent outside the stadium is a beer tent, and it's clearly very popular.

Left: London Road on rugby days is filled with fans making their pilgrimage to the match.

Right Top and Bottom: As part of the stadium complex can be found the London Marriott Hotel Twickenham, which in addition to its 144 rooms also has several suites, which must hold some of the best views in the world, for rugby fans at least, as they look out onto the pitch. Unfortunately, this opportunity was not open to me and my camera when I visited, as the ground was closed due to extra work being done in preparation for the World Cup.

Ever since 1878, the Army and the Navy have battled once a year in May at Twickenham Stadium. The match, known as 'Turf War' can be a very emotionally charged experience, as everyone playing has taken part in active service, and will have known someone to be injured or killed in the call of duty. The sense of camaraderie is strong for both teams, and these matches have become even more important since serving together in Afghanistan.

Thanks to Con O'Brien, local town centre manager for arranging this visit for me in 2014.

My thanks also to Jane Barron and Hannah Barrett from the RFU for allowing me to use these pictures.

The Stoop: Home of the Harlequins

Named after Adrian Stoop, long time player for the Harlequins, the Stoop Memorial Ground was built in 1963. It is now just called the Twickenham Stoop.

Adrian Stoop was only 22 when he was approached by both the Harlequins and Blackheath to play for them, whilst he was still at Oxford University and captain of the Rugby team. He captained Harlequins first ever international game at the Twickenham stadium, and revolutionised "Back Play".

The all-seater stadium consists of four stands and has a capacity of 14,800, making it the third largest dedicated rugby ground in the Aviva Premiership. The first match played at The Stoop was on November 23rd between Harlequins and Cambridge University. Since that match, Harlequins have played over 600 matches in the stadium. In May 2012, Harlequins were crowned Champions of England for the first time in their history, defeating Leicester Tigers in a gripping final at Twickenham Stadium.

Top left: Former Captain of Harlequins, and current Captain of the England team, Chris Robshaw, leads out his team for the last game of the 2014 season and what a nail-biter it was.

The last game of the season, Harlequins against Bath, was a very charged game; whoever won would get into the playoffs. Harlequins fans waved their team's colours, cheering as their team won the match and made it through.

Thanks to Ola Obaro, product marketing manager, for arranging my visit to the game.

Street Scenes

The streets of Twickenham have changed a lot since the rich upper classes moved into the area in the 1700's to build their mansions. What was once medieval farmland is now a bustling London town, far removed enough from the city to maintain its beautiful countryside feel. While the town itself is relatively small, many feel that the area of Twickenham stretches from Richmond Bridge all the way down to Strawberry Hill. This makes the area one of the most beautiful places in London, with its many parks, the beautiful old streets and big houses, and even the most commercialised roads are wide and welcoming to the travellers.

Because of its popularity with the elite historical figures in the past, the borough is teeming with local history. Many buildings can stake a claim to a long gone poet, artist or royal figure, or in the case of the area near Eel Pie Island, famous musicians. You never know who you might bump into around here, or if you might walk past the next great artist of our age.

Take a walk through the town and keep an eye on the architecture, especially when visiting the grand mansions. Many structures will have been built in one style, and extended, rebuilt or enhanced in a completely different theme, making fascinating buildings throughout the town.

Church Street

During the summer, Church street is closed to traffic from 6pm four nights a week for an Al Fresco dining experience.

Church Street takes its name from St Mary's Church at the top of Church Lane. Since Saxon times this route was the principal roadway uniting Richmond and Hampton. The street was first paved in 1716 with masonry rubble from the collapsed 15th century church nave. Traffic increased when Richmond Bridge was built in 1777, but reduced after 1899 when York Street was opened as the principal route. The history of Church Street and its assorted businesses represents the commercial and trading history of Twickenham where local families have lived and worked for generations.

As part of the Twickenham Festival, for a whole weekend Church street transformed into a French Market, with stalls lining the road, filled with delicious food.

Opposite Bottom Right and Left : Corto's Italian Deli on Church Street is one of the better Italian restaurants in the area. Corto himself can be seen in the picture on the left.

Church Street on an early Sunday morning becomes a very quiet road. You can't yet go for a drink, go shopping or attend a church service, but if you want to see the familiar street in a different light, this is the time to do it.

Below: Dating back to at least 1700, The Fox claims to be the oldest surviving pub in Twickenham.

Top left: Laura and Monty the labradoodle run the Kiss 'n' Make Up boutique on Church Street.

Bottom left: Bruce and his wife Hedda run Crusader Travel. Bruce is one of the most well regarded business people in the town and has run Twickenham Town Business Association for many years.

Bottom right: Rex the office dog from Milestone & Collis can often be found relaxing in the doorway, ready to welcome new customers.

Riverside

The road that stretches from the riverfront at Church Lane all the way to Marble Hill is simply called Riverside. It travels through Orleans Gardens, but never strays far from the water, and those that live along here are blessed with beautiful views, if a slight flooding problem. The White Swan rather handily puts out a chalk board letting visitors or just passers-by know what the tides will be doing that day.

Top: the rather impressive long boat found in the sandpit by the river.

Bottom: The footbridge over Riverside Road joins the two halves of York House gardens, an addition by Sir Ratan Tata during his stay.

Inset: Janet and her grandson enjoying a day out on the Riverside.

Built in the 17thC, the White Swan Pub boasts a good meal and a great view. Distanced perfectly between the town centre and the must see mansions, York House and Marble Hill House, this pub is the perfect location for a day out in Twickenham. Be careful, though; arrive at the wrong time of day and your meal in the garden might turn into a swim!

Opposite Top: Lebanon Park Road off of Riverside has a spectacular display of cherry trees in the spring.

Opposite bottom left: Also to be found in Lebanon Park is the Lebanon Park Dental Practice, run by Irena Blazewicz, and just happens to be where I have my teeth cared for. In her reception area you can find copies of all my books, so something nice to look forward to before she checks your teeth over.

Around 1720 the demand for houses in Twickenham was great enough to justify the building of two fine riverside terraces, both speculatively built by a Captain John Gray. By 1721 he had begun the construction of 24 houses in Montpelier Row and 10 in Sion Row. The houses in Sion Row are smaller than those in Montpelier Row, and have had fewer distinguished inhabitants, but they preserve much fine work and form an authentic part of old Twickenham.

Richmond Road

96

Top and bottom left: The Civic Centre for the London Borough of Richmond upon Thames was needing a wash on the day I visited, and the only way to get up that high is on a crane.

Top right: The Stokes and Moncrieff pub underwent some serious renovations in early 2014, transforming it into the welcoming establishment it is today. It is named after the leaders of the first ever international Rugby game in 1871, Frederik Stokes of England and Francis Moncrieff of Scotland.

Bottom right: The old Marble Hill pub narrowly escaped becoming a Sainsbury's, but was thankfully sold in 2012 to the new proprietors. Now named the Aleksander after their young son, the pub down the road from St Steven's church is a family friendly venue.

Montpelier Row

Built in the 1720s, this road has had many famous residents. Number 15 especially has a rich history: (Opposite bottom left) Poet Laureate Alfred Lord Tennyson lived here in the 1850s, and Pete Townshend of The Who owned the house from 1985 to 2008, and filmed a video inside. The house has a blue plaque and is listed due to its historical significance.

Based on Richmond Road, The Crown had a complete refurbishment in 2013 with the aim to highlight the beautiful Georgian architecture, and reopen the Victorian Hall at the back. They hold live acoustic nights every Thursday, Wine and Cider evenings, and even special menus for Rugby days.

Opposite: Buried in a backstreet, Oak Lane Cemetery was opened in 1838 when the churchyard of St Mary's Church was deemed too full to continue using. Buried here are WWI soldiers, contemporaries of Nelson and Wellington, the master of Trinity House, and the last Beadle of the Parish, but when it too filled up, it was closed in 1955. Friends of Oak Lane Cemetery restored the space in 2001, placing a central path and a side path through the area, and placing a gate at the entrance.

Surrounded by houses, this small area is a haven for natural wildlife in the area, as it is left mostly undisturbed. Those who live around it hear, instead of the usual street traffic noises, owls and foxes can in their nighttime ventures.

Bottom left: A Speckled-Wood butterfly sunning itself

London Road

Opposite: The Cabbage Patch pub, named after the affectionate nickname for Twickenham Rugby Stadium's humble beginnings, was opened in 1983. Sunday nights in the pub are especially popular, as it hosts very successful live music events regularly.

Top left: This Wetherspoon pub, the William Webb Ellis, is named after the founder of the Rugby World Cup, and opened in 2003.

Bottom left: The Albany pub, just off London Road, very popular on Rugby days.

Inset: Luluz Cafe is a particular favourite of my friend Con O'Brien, town centre manager for Richmond.

King Street

King Street, town centre for Twickenham, is undergoing a lot of improvements at the moment in an effort to make this part of the town less traffic dominated and more friendly to pedestrians and cyclists.

Laverstoke Park Farm is a butchers owned by Jodie Scheckter, an ex Formula 1 race driver. He owns his own farm, now, and sells his wares at this Twickenham shop.

Top right: Pip Chaney, the manageress, sells delicious meat, fresh mozzarella, gluton free sausages and buffalo milk ice cream.

Bottom left: The George Pub on King Street is a great spot for a drink. If you didn't manage to get tickets to the game, you can watch live here from the comfort of the sofas.

Sandy's Fishmongers is considered by many to be the best fish shop in Twickenham. They pride themselves on customer service and their fine produce, and try to stock as widely as possible to give the customers as much choice as they can.

As we went to press, disaster struck Sandy's by way of a burst water main that shot out a giant jet of water as high as their roof. Needless to say, the shop was seriously damaged, with all the fish being forcibly put back in water. To add insult to injury Sandy's had only just won the London in Bloom Business Premises of the Year.

Opposite top right: Outside Moidul's Rawalpindi Indian restaurant were the biggest display of flowers I have ever seen from a hanging basket.

Opposite bottom right: Stewart, the owner.

It might interest readers to know that Twickenham businesses came together early in 2014 to help better promote the businesses within the town. This new initiative, under the banner of 'Try Twickenham', is run for the businesses, by the businesses, and is all about showcasing the delightful independent traders and the numerous festivals, fairs, river events as well as Al Fresco that are all part of the Twickenham Fabric. All this and more is highlighted in this book and we fully support the efforts being made to promote Twickenham and in particular the 'Keep the Spend Local' theme. More information can be found at www.trytwickenham.com.

Heath Road

King Street splits after Wharf Lane, the left route becoming Cross Deep, and the right turn Heath Road. Follow this road along, past all the shops, and you will soon find Twickenham Green.

Top left: The newly refurbished Three Kings pub on Heath Road. With a pub quiz every Thursday night, and live bands every Saturday night, a good time can always be had here.

Twickenham Green

Twickenham Green is not an ancient village green but a surviving fragment of the eastern section of Hounslow Heath. Previously referred to as Twickenham Common or Little Common, the apex of the triangle may have been the sight of a pest house, where victims of infectious diseases such as smallpox or the plague were held. The water pump (see page 114), given for the use of the poor by Countess Waldegrave in 1894, marks the spot. By 1818, just over four acres of the Green was enclosed as the Workhouse Allotment, while to the south the properties were much grander, including Gifford Lodge and Twickenham Grange.

For more information on the Green please visit Friends of Twickenham Green – *www.twickenhamgreen.org*

Opposite: Holy Trinity is one of three churches on the green It is a Victorian Church, built in 1841, and contains an organ built by Henry Willis, one of England's most famous organ builders. The church has been expanded, rebuilt and changed a few times over the years.

This page: Friends of Twickenham Green held a fete on the 6th of July. The beautiful weather attracted a nice crowd, for whose entertainment one could find many typical stalls plus a beer tent from Twickenham Fine Ales and a stage featuring much live music.

Opposite top right: Commemorated here is the water pump that Countess Waldegrave installed for the use of the poor on the Green, and for the horse trough.

Opposite bottom: One of the tables outside Arthur's Bistro, found at the eastern end of the Green.

Right: Found in Mereway Road, just behind The Prince Blucher, the first brewery in almost a century in the area, Twickenham Fine Ales celebrated its tenth anniversary in 2014. One of their beers, the Sundancer, won the 2007 National Champion Beer of Britain.

Bottom: Built in 1845, this Fullers pub was named after a Field Marshall who helped the Duke of Wellington defeat Napoleon in the Battle of Waterloo. Renovated in 2014, it now has a heated terrace that is very popular on cooler days.

Squire's Garden Centre

When David Squire (always known as D.J.), Head Gardener and Groundsman for the Police Orphanage in Twickenham, was made redundant, he started up his own business, mainly landscaping small gardens. However, WWII began, and the landscaping stopped. The nurseries started growing vegetables instead and the company built Andersen air raid shelters for local people. After the war normal business resumed, but the way of life had changed, instead of hiring a gardener, by the 1960s many people did their own gardening. In 1964 Squire's opened their first garden in Twickenham, and the company has since expanded with 15 centres across the region. Squire's is still a family owned business, with D.J.'s son, Colin Squire, Chairman for the company, and his daughter Sarah as Deputy.

Schools

This page: St Catherine's School in Strawberry Hill was founded in 1914, taking lessons in the now demolished Orford Lodge. It was started for the middle class families in the area as a fee paying school and was run by nuns until 1991. The school moved in 1919 to the historic Pope's Villa, the former home of Alexander Pope.

Bottom Right: St Catherine's School shares the entrance to Alexander Pope's famous underground grotto with Radnor House School across the road (see page 8).

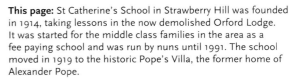

This page: Named after restorer of Strawberry Hill House, Frances Waldegrave, Waldegrave School was the result of the merging of two schools in 1980: Twickenham Girls and Kneller Girls. In September 2014 the School opened its Sixth Form and this included its first ever male students.

Opposite page: Still bearing the plaque from the Twickenham County School For Girls, Richmond Adult Community College offers adults the chance to continue their education. It started in the late 19th century when there few opportunities for children to attend secondary school, and after WWII started targeting older students.

Opposite right: RACC shares its buildings and some of the facilities with St Richard Reynolds School.

This page: Orleans Park School opened in 1973, tucked between York House Gardens and Marble Hill. The building was extended in 1993, and in 2014 the school opened a Sixth Form. Former attendees include student Josh Herdman, who also attended Hogwarts as Gregory Goyle, and teacher Greg Davies, who played Mr Gilbert in 'The Inbetweeners'.

Strawberry Hill

Horace Walpole discovered 'Chopped-Straw Hill' in 1747, one of the few remaining spaces on the Thames in the popular Twickenham area. Here he created the gothic Strawberry Hill House, complete with battlements and a round tour in the meadows. This house was a novelty and a tourist attraction, even at the time, and guided tours were lead round the house, and it was host to royal parties. It spawned a new trend towards gothic themes in architecture and literature, when previously people had so enjoyed classic symmetry and neatness in architecture. It was here that Walpole published and printed his first gothic novel, The Castle of Ontrato.

The house was inherited by Lady Waldegrave in 1811. Her second husband, the Second Earl Waldegrave, was sent to prison for riotous behaviour, and as an act of revenge towards Twickenham he sold Walpole's precious collection and decided to leave the house to rot. However, when he died in 1846, Lady Waldegrave set to work on the house, extending it and building grand rooms, and pushing the main road back to where it lies now.

Strawberry Hill House

The Gothic architecture, while seen most clearly in the daylight, is enchanting in the mist, thematically fitting Walpole's vision.

Strawberry Hill house held Twickenham Family Fun Day, organised by Twickenham Alive, inviting the public to spend the first weekend of the summer holidays on the grounds.

While the rail line has been here since 1863, it took another ten years for Strawberry Hill station to be built. From this spot on the level crossing, you can look north up the track for miles.

Strawberry Hill Golf Club

Strawberry Hill Golf Club began in 1900, when the Chiswick Golf Club was sold for housing, so one of the members offered their own property as a new venue. It took some time before it was suitable for the purpose, but the Golf Club has stayed on the property ever since. To celebrate the 100 year anniversary of the Club, a centenary oak tree was planted by the mayor between the 1st and 9th fairway.

On the 21st April 2014, Easter Monday, they held an Open Day, which was sponsored by amongst others Milestone & Collis. Thank you to Alan Plumb for inviting me along.

Radnor Gardens

Josh Robartes lived on these grounds between 1722 and 1757, and the house was named after his title, 4th Earl of Radnor. Purchased in 1906 by the Urban District Council, the house remained here until bomb damage in the war. A stream used to cut through the parallel to the river but was silted over in 1965, though the bridge has been left to mark the track.

From Radnor Gardens you can see down the river to Eel Pie Island, and past the bridge St Mary's Church is easily visible. The area is very popular for dog walking, and given half a chance the dogs will run in the water for a swim.

Friends of Radnor Gardens aim to keep improving the park, to make it more accessible to the general public and improve quality of life in the area.

www.friendsofradnorgardens. org.uk

Bottom right: The Alexander Pope Hotel was built in 1852 as a pub by Young's on part of Alexander Pope's old garden, but it was destroyed by bombs in the Second World War and the present building was opened in 1959. It was completely refurbished and upgraded in 2000 into a hotel with 32 bedrooms.

East Twickenham

Most of East Twickenham lies either on what used to be Twickenham Park or Cambridge Park. The boundaries of Twickenham Park were first established by Richard, Earl of Cornwall in 1227, enclosing it from the surrounding heath. The boundaries, owners and uses of the park changed a lot over the years, 16thC philosopher Sir Francis Bacon owned the estate for a while, but in 1840 the development of villas began, leading to the residential filling in that covers the land today.

In WWI, East Twickenham had a very different community than today. Charles Pelabon, a French man but owner of a Belgian factory, moved to England during the war, opening a munitions factory in a disused roller skating rink. Belgians, seeking refuge from Europe as Germany invaded, flocked to the factory for work, and East Twickenham became established as a real Belgian community, the neighbourhood becoming known as 'le village belge sur la Tamise'. Hiring 2000 men and women, the streets would flood with workers when the shifts changed, visiting the newly opened Belgian shops and buying copies of the specially sold L'Indepence Belge. However, at the end of the war, the community promptly packed up and returned home, and this chapter of the area has been all but forgotten.

Richmond Bridge
GATEWAY TO EAST TWICKENHAM

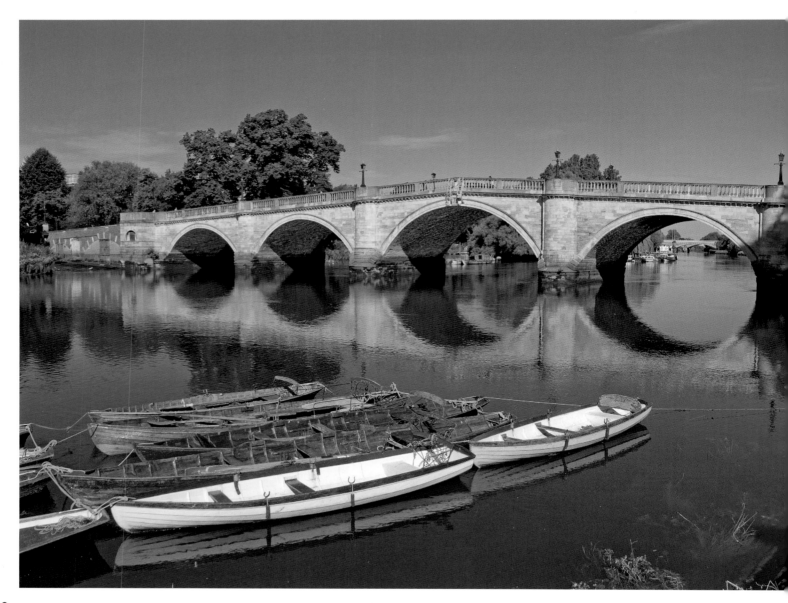

Opened in 1777, Richmond Bridge was built as a replacement for the ferrys that carried commuters between Twickenham and Richmond. Due to the growing population requiring transport, and the service being unreliable because of weather conditions, the need for a permanent crossing from Henry VII's Richmond Palace to Twickenham park was met.

Left: Grey herons wait on the river bank for lunch, or perhaps for a ferry.

Previous page: Cambridge Gardens are part of the old grounds of Cambridge house, a 17thC mansion. Sir Edward Dean Paul, an inheritor of the estate, angered the Twickenham Local Board by erecting railings on either side of a path on the estate to prevent people from entering. In 1907, the estate began to be built over, separating the mansion from the river, and the building became a hotel, and in 1937 was eventually demolished.

This page: In June, Cambridge Gardens threw a summer fair. Hosted by Friends Of East Twickenham, the day features pony rides, bouncy castles, and for the adults a beer tent and taster tennis sessions. For more information on the work of the Friends please visit *www.easttwickenham.org*

Left: Willoughby House, a 19thC villa, was formerly known as Caen House. Its symmetrical tower is mirrored on the other side of the river by the tower above the Pitcher & Piano.

Right: Ryde House was built at around the same time as Willoughby House, and is a very striking house on the street. These houses were some of the first housing developments on Cambridge Park.

Bottom: Richmond Road looking east towards Richmond Bridge and into the town named after a palace built by Henry VII.

Top: Richmond Bridge club holds court in the old Richmond Bowls pavilion in Cambridge Gardens.

Bottom: Some of the houses on Rosslyn Road and Riverdale Gardens display some quite exotic architecture; one lodge of the Twickenham Park estate still exists here.

Opposite: Hatfield House in Cambridge Park.

Richmond Lock, just visible in the far distance, built in 1894 is a pedestrian bridge connecting Richmond with St Margaret's. Twickenham Railway Bridge and the lock are both Grade II listed structures.

Twickenham Bridge, visible between the arches, was opened on 3 July 1933 by the Prince of Wales. The architect was Maxwell Ayrton, who first envisaged four 70 foot towers to be constructed on the riverbanks with retaining walls of 20 feet above road level. The plans were widely opposed and a local petition was organised by the Daily Telegraph on the grounds that it was inappropriate to the setting. The final design of the bridge of three reinforced-concrete arches supported on concrete piers with Art Deco lamps and open bronzework embellishments is what we see today. The bridge incorporates three permanent hinges enabling the structure to adjust to changes in temperature, the first reinforced concrete bridge structure in the UK to use such an innovation.

Far right: Asgill House

Thanks to George for allowing me on his houseboat to take this picture on Ducks Walk.

St Margarets

Before the railway arrived here, St Margarets was little more than a house, the summer home of Lord Cassilis, Marquis of Ailsa, and later owned by the Earl of Kilmorey. Walking around the area, you can still see this commemorated in street names such as Kilmorey Gardens and Ailsa Road. The town was one of the first garden suburbs, and many Victorian houses still remain from the development of the estate. The artist JMW Turner built a house here, which still stands today. Initially called Solus Lodge, it now stands as Sandycoombe Lodge in Sandycoombe Road. A Grade II listed Georgian Mansion, Gordon House, built in 1814, and has been partially used as a University and as housing. The mausoleum of the 2nd Earl of Kilmorey and his mistress lies in the North of St Margarets in the style of an ancient Egyptian monument. Bordered by the Thames and the River Crane, this sweet town has beautiful local walks for those lucky enough to live here.

Opposite: Twickenham Bridge (background) and Twickenham Railway Bridge (foreground)

St Margarets station was
built in 1876 on the existing
trainline from Waterloo to
Windsor.

Top right: Zoran Deli on Crown Road serves the hungry locals breakfast, lunch and dinner, as well as catering delicious food for events.

Inset: Denham & Finney gift shop

Bottom right: Darren (right) and Leigh (left) Armstrong from Armstrongs Butchers on St Margarets Road won the Best Bangers Competition in Jubilee Gardens (page 67) with a family recipe passed down for 80 years.

Opposite and above:
Arguably Britain's best landscape painter, JMW Turner, built a retreat here for himself and his father two hundred years ago. Still standing today, the house is now used as a museum about Turner and his work.

As we go to press, Turner is about to be celebrated in a new film by Mike Leigh, featuring by all accounts a towering performance by Timothy Spall as Turner.

Clockwise from top left:
Built on a former ice rink, Twickenham Studios was established in 1913, and was, at the time, the UK's largest film studios.

All Hallows Church on the A316, Chertsey Road, is iconic for travellers on their journey out of London.

This church signals the beginning of the countryside to many. Constructed in 1940 using parts from other churches, mainly All Hallows Lombard Street, which was destroyed by a fire. During the consecration ceremony in 1939, gunfire could be heard.

The effort put into the interior of St Margarets pub is astounding: the wooden floors, ornate chandeliers and brickwork all creates an atmosphere that welcomes and amazes the customers.

This odd looking building on the corner of St Margaret's Road and Rosslyn Road is the surviving 19th century gate lodge for Twickenham Park Estate.

Pleasure Gardens

This page and overleaf: These beautiful gardens are one of London's best kept secrets. With entry only available to those that back directly onto the 12 acres of enclosed space, it is a haven to all that live there, providing a safe community space for the neighbourhood.

The Gardens are run by a commitee of residents and thanks to John Ward the chairman of the committee for letting me in to take these pictures.

These gardens are hidden behind St Peter's Road (pictured top right), St George's Road and Ailsa Road.

Moormead

In 1893 a local paper wrote about how a recreation ground in the area would be financially desirable, and that it would provide a "place for healthy exercise and the promotion of clean lives". Five years later, Moormead opened the park as a recreation area, and has been used for sports ever since, with a children's playground, a pavilion, and space for football and cricket.

Bottom right: Run by the St Margarets Fair Committee, this community event held each July raises money for local charities.

Open Spaces

Now part of London, Twickenham was not all that long ago completely one big open space. In the 1700s, as the rich and upper class Londoners started to move out here to create large mansions on the riverfront, the land became split up into estates and parks, such as Twickenham and Cambridge park. The population followed the expansion of the city and the train line to the area, so the once never ending countryside slowly began to be filled over by housing, businesses and industry. Today the parks are much smaller, little blissful oases between the buildings, or long sprawling riverside walks. Being on the edge of the city and the countryside, Twickenham is blessed to have the choice between the two worlds.

Orleans House and Gardens

Built in 1710 by John James for the politician and diplomat James Johnston, the house was actually not named Orleans until Louis Philippe Duc d'Orleans rented the house in the early 1800s, before he became King of France. Much of the House has now been demolished, as it was broken apart and sold in 1910, but the remaining intact pieces were bought and saved, before passing into the property of the borough. The site now holds an art gallery, a café and an education centre.

The gardens were at the centre of a recent local controversy, now dropped, when it was muted that it should be the site for housing The Queen's barge *Gloriana* – possibly a shame, as it would have been a great visitor attraction for the area but seeing both sides, much of the park would would have gone too.

Orleans House can be hired out for weddings, just like this happy couple have done. In August 2014, they got married here and rowed down the river, courtesy of Hammerton's Ferry, to their reception at Petersham.

Ham Lands

This 72 hectare open space is primarily a flood plane, but on the drier months the grasslands are perfect for a long walk along the Thames. In the early 20thC it was excavated for gravel, and was filled back in with soil from different parts of London, and with bomb rubble from WWII. Because of the variety in the soil, and the alkaline rubble, it became a very diverse natural habitat for many different animals and plants. Some of the vegetation in the preserved Ham Lands is very unusual for London, making it a very important wildlife habitat.

Left: The New Southern Belle, one of Turk Launches large fleet of cruise vessels, is a regular sight along this stretch of the river. Turk Launches are based in Kingston and operate between Richmond and Hampton Court.

Wildlife like this lone coot are drawn to the Ham Lands because of the diverse habitat.

Hammerton's Ferry

Previous spread: Hammerton's Ferry

Hammerton's Ferry is a family owned business taking commuters from Marble Hill to Ham House across the river. Started in 1908, the business almost ended then; before 1902, the Ham House land was privately owned, and therefore there was no need for such a service, but when it was sold, and Walter Hammerton began the public service, his competitors in Twickenham Ferry took them to court. Winning the case, Hammerton Ferry has outlasted the other company, and survives to this day.

Opposite top right: Francis, director of Hammerton's and his son Andy.

You don't have to use a ferry to cross the river; many residents take to the river themselves with their own boats, or in this case, a kayak.

Marble Hill Park

The Twickenham area was considered a perfect location by the rich and powerful, as it was close to London, but upstream on the Thames from the noise and pollution of the inner city. Marble Hill House, built in the 1720s, is a Palladian Villa built originally for Henrietta Howard, mistress of King George II. It was built by Roger Morris and Architect Henry Herbert, 9th Earl of Pembroke, and their creation was so beloved that it became the inspiration for the Georgian Architecture that was so popular across the Colonies, becoming a model for many houses.

Henrietta Howard was beloved by the public, despite her scandalous position as a mistress instead of wife, but Queen Caroline of Ansbach, wife of George II, was fond of her and was glad her husband had picked such an agreeable mistress. Henrietta had many historically significant friends, such as Alexander Pope, Johnathan Swift and John Gay who all came to visit her frequently at the House, and she has been immortalised in literature such as in *The Rape of the Lock* by Pope and Sir Walter Scott's *Heart of the Midlothian*.

The House and its grounds, after a failed effort to sell it for housing developments, was sold for public use in 1902, and a year later it was open for all to see. After refurbishment to bring it back to its former beauty, the house and its gardens have many amenities such as tennis courts, cafes, children's play areas and hosts events, such as the Jazz Café.

This Eastern Black Walnut
stands in the grounds on
Marble Hill House as a
centerpiece on the great
lawn. While beautiful in
the summer, adorned with
leaves, during the winter the
great bare branches look very
dramatic silhouetted against
the fog or the sky.

The open grounds are perfect for dog walking.

Bottom right and opposite:
The display of dafodills in the
spring can be spectacular.

York House Gardens

York House and its gardens lies on the river, very central in the town. Almost directly opposite Eel Pie Island, it's the perfect venue for a day out without straying far from Church Street.

On the grounds in front of the Naked Ladies statue collection the local amateur dramatics society held Shakespeare in the Park.

Overleaf: York House, now used by the council including the Mayor's Parlour and Council Chamber.

The Naked Ladies were part of a collection, acquired by Sir Ratan Tata after the suicide of the original owner. Not knowing how the collection was originally intended, the layout was largely guesswork, which is why many claim that the positions of some of the women are unusual. In WWII, due to concerns that the shining marble would be a landmark for German bombers, they were covered in 'grey sludge'. Falling into disrepair by the 1980s there was a chance that they were going to be left to rot. Through the efforts of some local people, they were restored and re-emerged in 1989 good as new. Requiring constant attention, they may soon require another rallying call to help with their upkeep.

Thank you to the Twickenham Museum for the background on these beautiful objects.

Contrary to other houses of the same name, Twickenham's York House was not named after a Duke of York, but instead after a farming family named Yorke, land owners of the area. Parts of the house date back to the 1630s, and it has been altered and refurbished many times over the centuries. The last private owner of the house before Twickenham Council acquired it was Indian Industrialist Sir Ratan Tata, who owned it from 1906 until his death in 1918, and his extensive modifications to the gardens remain today. He lowered the lawn to make an Italian Lawn, a very popular style for garden parties, created a Japanese Garden, and acquired the Naked Ladies statue collection.

Above: During the winter of 2013, Twickenham Alive erected an ice rink on the tennis courts, proving to be very popular.

Crane Valley

The beautiful Crane Valley has changed a lot over the years. Once a very dangerous area to live near and work in, residents frequently use it as a walk to the shops. The one remaining intact building in the park is the shot tower, used as a lookout post for fires.

On the former site of the Hounslow Gunpowder Mills, Crane park and valley is now a long park and nature reserve following the River Crane's route. The mill opened in the 1760s and was reputed to have the finest black gunpowder in Europe. When walking through the park, as many locals do daily as a shortcut to the shops, you can still see evidence of the factory, such as the mill streams and the machine wheels, but also large mounds that enclosed the small workshops where the gunpowder was ground. Strict security measures were in place, but it often wasn't enough; there was a total of 55 explosions on the site, including one that many Londoners mistook for an earthquake in 1722, destroying three mills and damaging Horace Walpole's house in Strawberry Hill, two miles away. In 1927 the site ceased being active, as the increased population in the area due to the train line being extended was becoming an increasing safety hazard.

Run by the London Wildlife Trust, the Crane Valley also has a thriving Nature Reserve, based on an island opposite the tower. It is famous for its Banded Demoiselle Damselflies in the summer, but many different types of animal can be found here (frogs, their spawn and squirrels amongst them). This area is a beautiful example of what can be done with a grant from the Lottery Fund by a few inspired people.

Local walk

HOW TO TRULY EXPERIENCE TWICKENHAM

We felt it would be nice to incorporate a walk so that you can truly experience the beauty and history of the area for yourself. Here you will find details on one of the many walks around the area. The map (opposite) can also be found on the dust jacket of this book. A full detailed guide to the walk can be found on our website to download as an A4 sheet: *www.unity-publishing.co.uk*. You can complete this historical walk independently, or you can travel with either Discovery Richmond or Richmond Heritage Guides, who both promote this walk and others in this area. We can only fit so much on our walk sheet, so if you want to experience the walk in more detail, why not join the professional guides from Discovery Richmond or Richmond Heritage Guides. Discovery Richmond run year round, making sure to give you the best version of the route whatever the season, keeping track of museum and house opening hours, and can be found at *www.discoveryrichmond.com*. Richmond Heritage Guides run from June to October, making the most of the summer months, and start from the other end at St Mary's Church; they can be found at *www.richmondwalks.co.uk*.

Starting at Strawberry Hill Station, this walk incorporates some of the most historically significant areas of Twickenham, and also some of the most beautiful. After passing Twickenham Studios (1), you can visit Turner's House (2), before walking past Marble Hill House (3). You can take a detour into the grounds, or even visit the house, before coming back to the road and taking a look at Montpelier Row (4) and walking down the riverfront to Orleans House (5), and visiting the Octagonal Gallery (6). The next stop is York House Gardens (7), taking a peek at the Naked Ladies, and then back onto the river through the church grounds (8). Lastly, you can walk across Eel Pie Bridge (9) to take a look at the iconic island, and finish the walk in the heart of Twickenham (10), maybe for something to eat or drink in one of the many cafes or pubs.

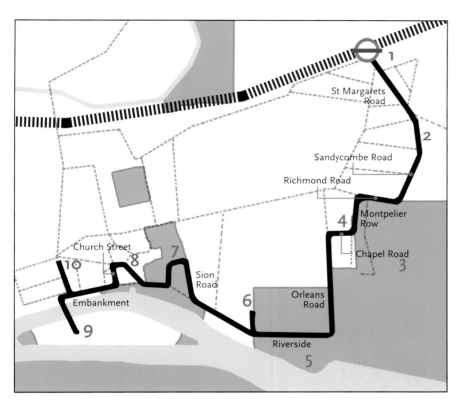

Opposite left: River front and Eel Pie Island

Opposite right: The new Bug Hotel on the Embankment

Top right: The courtyard cafe at Orleans House, a great place to stop for a break

Bottom left: The Naked Ladies at York House Gardens with Dial House in the background

Bottom right: Marble Hill House and park

All rights reserved. No part of this publication may be reproduced, stored in any retrieval system or transmitted in any form or by any means, electronic, mechanical photocopying or otherwise without the prior permission of the copyright holders. Whilst every care has been taken in the production of this book, no responsibility can be accepted for any errors or omissions. The publishers have taken all reasonable care in compiling this work but cannot accept responsibility for the information derived from third parties, which has been reproduced in good faith.

First Edition – © Unity Print and Publishing Limited 2014

Designed by Ball Design Consultancy
www.balldesignconsultancy.com

Proofread by Tom Sears
www.tom-sears.com

Printed by Page Brothers of Norwich, Norfolk.
www.pagebros.co.uk

Colour Management by Paul Sherfield of The Missing Horse Consultancy.
www.missinghorsecons.co.uk

Publishing Assistant: Jessica Dean

Published by Unity Print and Publishing Limited,
18 Dungarvan Avenue,
London SW15 5QU.
Tel: +44 (0)20 8487 2199
aw@unity-publishing.co.uk
www.unity-publishing.co.uk

Follow Andrew on Twitter:
@andrewpics